M000020248

Heinemann
First
Encyclopedia

Volume 4
Eye-Hip

Heinemann Library
Chicago, Illinois

© 1999 Reed Educational & Professional Publishing
Published by Heinemann Library,
an imprint of Reed Educational & Professional Publishing,
Chicago, IL 60602
Customer Service: 888-454-2279
Visit our website at www.heinemannlibrary.com

Series Editors: Rebecca and Stephen Vickers
Author Team: Rob Alcraft, Catherine Chambers, Jim Drake,
Fred Martin, Angela Royston, Jane Shuter, Roger Thomas,
Rebecca Vickers, Stephen Vickers

Photo research by Katharine Smith
Designed and Typeset by Gecko Ltd
Printed in Hong Kong, China

03 02 01 00
10 9 8 7 6 5 4 3 2

Library of Congress Cataloging-in-Publication Data

Heinemann first encyclopedia.
    p.   cm.
    Summary: A ten-volume encyclopedia covering animals, plants,
countries, transportation, science, ancient civilizations, and world
history.
    ISBN 1-57572-741-2 (lib. bdg.)
    1. Children's encyclopedias and dictionaries. [1. Encyclopedias
and dictionaries.] I. Heinemann Library (Firm)
AG5.H45   1998
031—dc21   98-20016
                                                               CIP
                                                               AC

Acknowledgments
Cover: The cover illustration is of a male specimen of Ornithoptera goliath, commonly called the Goliath Birdwing. Special thanks to
Dr. George C. McGavin and the Hope Entomological Collections, Oxford University Museum of Natural History; J. Allan Cash Ltd,
pp. 7 top, 9, 17, 26, 28, 29, 34, 35, 36, 47; Ancient Art and Architecture/Mary Jelcliffe, p. 46; Ardea London Ltd/J.M. Labat, p. 12
bottom; Valerie Taylor, p. 12 top; Bridgeman Art Library, p. 5; BBC Natural History Unit/John Cancalosi, p. 22 top; Jeff Rotman,
p. 11 bottom; Trevor Clifford Photography, pp. 24, 42 bottom; Bruce Coleman/Wayne Larkinen, p. 45 top; FLPA/Fritz Polking, p.
10 bottom; Ronald Grant Archive/Walt Disney Co., p. 6 bottom; Hulton Deutsch, p. 44 top; The Hutchison Library/Sarah
Errington, p. 38; Oxford Scientific Films/Jen and Den Bartlett, p. 32; G.I. Bernard, p. 25 bottom; Mike Birkhead, p. 45 bottom;
Roger Brown, p. 27 bottom; George Bruce, p. 18; Alan and Sandy Carey, p. 23 bottom; Bruce Davidson, p. 48 top; Tim Davis, p. 30
top; Mark Deebie and Victoria Stone, p. 14 top; Jack Dermid, p. 25 top; Paul Franklin, p. 21 top; Jim Frazer, p. 40 bottom; David
Fritts, p. 31 bottom; Christian Gazimek, p. 20; Mike Hill, p. 14 bottom; Tim Jackson, p. 30 bottom; Paul Kay, p. 37 bottom; Michael
Leach, p. 4; Renee Lynn, p. 23 top; Alistair MacEwen, p.15; Sean Morris, p. 33 bottom; Owen Newman, p. 43; Richard Parkwood,
p. 48 bottom; Hans Reinhard, p. 21 bottom; James Robinson, p. 31 top; Survival Anglia/T. Andrewartha, p. 39 bottom; Survival
Anglia/Claude Steelman, p. 39 top; Charles Tyler, p. 7 bottom; Peter Ward, p. 27 top; Martin Wendler, p. 33 top; M. Wilding, p. 40
top; Redferns, p. 19; Science Photo Library/Agema Infrared Systems, p. 42 top; Deep Light Industries, p. 41; Simon Fraser, p. 8; Tony
Stone Worldwide/Ary Diesendruck, p. 16 top; Alan Hicks, p. 44 bottom; Alan Thornton, p. 13; Sygma, p. 16.

Welcome to
Heinemann First Encyclopedia

What is an encyclopedia?

An encyclopedia is an information book. It gives the most important facts about many different subjects. This encyclopedia has been written for children who are using an encyclopedia for the first time. It covers many of the subjects from school and others you may find interesting.

What is in this encyclopedia?

In this encyclopedia, each topic is called an *entry*. There is one page of information for every entry. The entries in this encyclopedia explain

- animals
- plants
- dinosaurs
- countries
- geography
- history
- world religions
- music
- art
- transportation
- science
- technology

How to use this encyclopedia

This encyclopedia has eleven books called *volumes*. The first ten volumes contain entries. The entries are all in alphabetical order. This means that Volume 1 starts with entries that begin with the letter *A* and Volume 10 ends with entries that begin with the letter *Z*. Volume 11 is the index volume. It also has interesting information about American history.

Here are two entries that show you what you can find on a page:

The "see also" line tells you where to find other related information.

This is the letter that the entry starts with.

Fact boxes give you details about the topic.

Did You Know? boxes have fun or interesting bits of information.

The Fact File tells you important facts and figures.

Eye

see also: Animals, Human Body

Eyes are the parts of the body through which humans and animals see. Light bounces off objects. The light makes an image of an object. Eyes catch the light to see the image. Most parts of the human eye are kept safe inside the head.

Eye problems

When the lens of the eye is the wrong shape, the eye cannot focus. Glasses and contact lenses help eyes to focus.

DID YOU KNOW?

Animals that hunt at night have special pupils in their eyes. The pupils open very wide. This lets in as much light as possible.

The owl has big pupils. Big pupils help the owl to see in the dark.

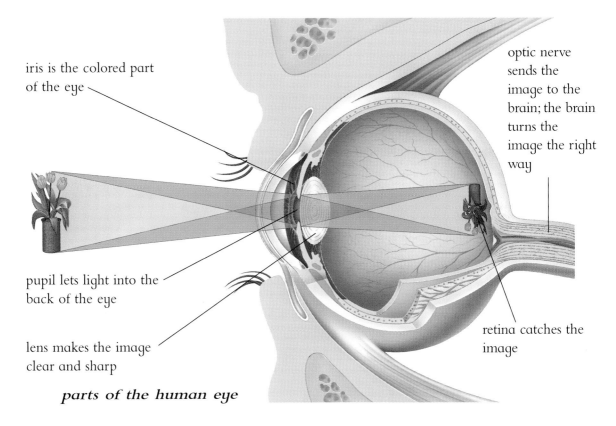

iris is the colored part of the eye

optic nerve sends the image to the brain; the brain turns the image the right way

pupil lets light into the back of the eye

lens makes the image clear and sharp

retina catches the image

parts of the human eye

Fable

see also: Legend, Literature, Myth, Story

A fable is a short story. It teaches a lesson. The lesson is called a moral. The characters in a fable are usually animals. The animals behave and talk like people.

Who wrote fables?

The most well-known fable storytellers and writers are Aesop, Jean de la Fontaine, and Gotthold Ephraim Lessing. Aesop lived in ancient Greece about 2,500 years ago. He probably was a slave on the island of Samos. Fontaine lived in France in the 1800s. Lessing lived in Germany about 100 years after Fontaine. Their stories are translated into many languages.

This illustration was made more than 200 years ago. It is for the fable "The Fox and the Grapes."

DID YOU KNOW?

In one of Aesop's fables, the fox finds an actor's mask. The mask has holes for the eyes and mouth. "Ah!" says the fox to the mask, "You are beautiful on the outside, but behind your face there is nothing!" The moral is that people should not worry about how they look. They should think about the way they behave.

BIDPAI

A wise man named Bidpai wrote a collection of animal fables. He lived in India about 1,500 years ago. Bidpai used fables to tell how a young prince should lead his life.

Fairy Tale

see also: Fable, Literature, Myth, Story

Fairy tales are children's stories. The stories have been told for hundreds of years. Not all fairy tales are about fairies. Usually they are about magic or imaginary creatures. Some fairy tales are about times long ago. Some fairy tales are about present times.

Who wrote fairy tales?

Some of the most well-known fairy tales are from the Grimm Brothers. They published a book of fairy tales in the 1800s. Hans Christian Andersen lived in Denmark in the 1800s. He wrote 150 fairy tales. He wrote "Thumbelina," a story about a tiny girl.

Hans Christian Andersen wrote many well-known stories. He wrote "The Princess and the Pea" and "The Ugly Duckling."

Jacob Grimm (1785–1863)

Wilhelm Grimm (1786–1859)

The Grimm Brothers collected old fairy tales. The tales were hundreds of years old. They wrote the stories in a book called *Tales from the Brothers Grimm*. Two of these stories are "Hansel and Gretel" and "Snow White."

The Grimm Brothers' fairy tale "Snow White" was made into an animated movie.

Farming

see also: Crop, Soil, Weather

Farming is the work people do to grow crops and provide food. In some places, farmers and their families eat most of what they grow. In other places, farmers grow crops to sell to other people.

Types of farming

Farmers grow grain, fruit, and vegetables to eat. They also grow cotton, tobacco, or flowers. These crops are used to make things. Farmers also raise animals.

Fields in Nepal are flooded with water. Then rice plants are planted by hand.

Big machinery like this combine helps farmers harvest huge crops.

People and farming

People have farmed for more than nine thousand years. Some farm work is done by hand. Pitchforks, hoes, and spades are hand tools. Machinery also does farm work. Tractors pull plows. Balers bundle hay.

Some farmers use chemicals. Fertilizers help the crops grow. Insecticides and pesticides control or kill weeds and insects. Some farming is organic farming. Organic farms do not use chemicals.

DID YOU KNOW?

More people in the world do farming work than any other kind of work.

Fern

see also: Plants

A fern is a green plant. It does not have flowers. Ferns grow in most parts of the world. They grow best in damp, shady places. They do not grow in deserts.

Life of a fern

Ferns produce spores. They do not produce seeds. The wind blows the spores around. A spore falls to the ground. It grows into a small leaf. It is shaped like a heart. The leaf has male and female seeds. A new fern grows when a male seed and a female seed are joined.

Ferns were one of the first plants to grow on land. Millions of years ago, giant tree ferns covered much of the land. Today people grow ferns in their gardens. Ferns are also house plants.

FERN FACTS

NUMBER OF KINDS	about 10 thousand
HEIGHT	1 inch to 82 feet
LIFE SPAN	up to 100 years
ENEMIES	animals that eat ferns

Tree ferns are the largest ferns. They grow in hot, tropical countries. Tree ferns are one of the oldest types of plants still alive.

a frond of a lady fern

The leaf of a fern is called a frond. It has many smaller leaves with leaflets. Spores are found on the underside of the leaflets.

Finland

see also: Arctic, Europe

Finland is a country in northern Europe. The land is mostly low and flat. It has some hills and mountains in the north. There are many lakes and forests. Summers are warm. Winters are very cold and snowy.

Living in Finland

Most Finns live in cities in the south. People in the country live in traditional houses made of wood. Finns eat potatoes with meat or fish. The fish is often herring.

Farmers grow grain and root crops. Reindeer are raised for meat. Fish are caught and processed around the coast. Many people work in factories. The factories make paper and other things from wood.

The *kantele* is a stringed instrument played in Finland. Poetry is read as it is played.

Laplanders handle boats well. These people are wearing traditional clothing.

DID YOU KNOW?

Lapland is in the north of Finland. The people of Lapland herd reindeer and catch fish.

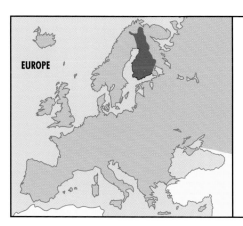

EUROPE

FACT FILE

PEOPLE	Finnish, Finns
POPULATION	about 5 million
MAIN LANGUAGES	Finnish, Swedish
CAPITAL CITY	Helsinki
MONEY	Euro
HIGHEST MOUNTAIN	Haltiatunturi–4,345 feet
LONGEST RIVER	Kemijoki River–340 miles

Firefly

see also: Beetle, Insect

A firefly is an insect. Fireflies are beetles that give off a glowing or flashing light. Fireflies are often called lightning bugs. They live all over the world. They do not live in Antarctica.

Firefly families

The female lays eggs in damp soil. The eggs hatch into glowworms. Each glowworm eats and grows for about two years. Then it changes into a pupa. Finally it changes into a firefly. An adult firefly lives from a few days to a month.

FIREFLY FACTS

NUMBER OF KINDS	1,900
COLOR	brown or black with red, yellow, or orange markings
LENGTH	less than an inch
STATUS	common
LIFE SPAN	up to 2 years
ENEMIES	birds, lizards, frogs, spiders

the underside of a Jamaican firefly

soft, but tough skin to protect the body

yellowy-green light to attract a mate; each kind of firefly has its own light

hard wing case to cover and to protect the wings

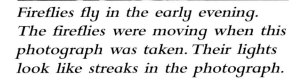

Fireflies fly in the early evening. The fireflies were moving when this photograph was taken. Their lights look like streaks in the photograph.

PLANT AND INSECT EATER

A glowworm eats flowers, snails, earthworms, and caterpillars. It kills its food with its poison. Some adult fireflies do not eat at all. Others feed on nectar. Nectar is a sweet juice made by some flowers.

Fish

see also: Fish, Tropical; Sea Life

A fish is an animal with fins, gills, and a backbone. Many fish have sharp teeth. Fish live wherever there is water. They live almost everywhere in the world. Many fish live in seas and oceans. Other fish live in ponds, lakes, rivers, and streams.

FISH FACTS

NUMBER OF KINDS	more than 20 thousand
COLOR	all colors and patterns
LENGTH	half inch to 39 feet
WEIGHT	up to 17 tons
STATUS	common
LIFE SPAN	up to 50 years
ENEMIES	other fish, squid, people

Fish families

A female fish lays her eggs in the water. The eggs hatch. Then the young fish eat the egg yolk until they can find their own food. Most young fish are called fry.

back and anal fins to keep from rolling over

gills to take in oxygen from water

tail and tail fin that move from side to side and push the fish through water

hard scales to protect the body

fins to steer through water

a cod

Some fish live on their own. Other fish swim in big groups called schools.

PLANT, INSECT, AND MEAT EATER

Most fish eat other fish and sea animals. Many fish have sharp teeth. Some fish feed on water plants. Fish also eat tiny plants and animals called plankton.

Fish, Tropical

see also: Coral, Fish, Sea Life

Tropical fish are small, colorful fish. They live in warm waters in South America, Africa, and southern Asia. Many people keep tropical fish as pets.

Tank life

Pet fish live in water tanks called aquariums. Only fish that like the same kind of water can live together in the same tank. Most tropical fish like warm water. Some tropical fish like cooler water. Some tropical fish can only live in salt water. Some tropical fish are very fierce. Piranhas are so fierce that they have to be kept away from other fish.

Aquarium fish eat dried fish food. The tank must be kept clean. The tank must be big enough for the fish.

Tropical fish are found in the wild. These fish live near a coral reef.

small heater keeps the water at the correct temperature

plants and stones give fish places to hide

air bubbles give fish oxygen to breathe

an aquarium for tropical fish

Flag

see also: Communication

A flag is a piece of cloth. It has colored patterns, shapes, or symbols on it. Flags are flown from ropes, poles, or sticks. Flags may hang down from buildings. People have used flags for more than a thousand years. Flags are a way of saying something without using words.

The sailor uses two flags to send a message. The positions of the flags stand for the letters of the alphabet. This flag alphabet is called semaphore.

FLAG FIRSTS

1777 ..... American flag is first used— the number of stars changed over time

1801 ..... modern British flag, the Union Jack, is first used

1857 ..... flags are first used for international ship signaling

1863 ..... Red Cross flag is first used

1901 ..... modern Australian flag is first used

1914 ..... Olympic flag with five linking circles is first used.

1948 ..... United Nations flag is first used

Using flags

Countries, groups, clubs, and teams have flags. Flags say, "This is ours." Flags say, "This is who we stand for."

Armies used to carry flags into battle. An army won when it captured its opponent's flag.

Ships use special flags to signal to each other. Flags give messages even when the ship's crew does not speak the same language.

A ship that is in trouble will hang its flag upside down. This lets others know that the ship is in trouble.

Flags in motor racing signal "start," "finish," and "danger on the roadway." Everyone in the race understands the flag signals.

Flamingo

see also: Bird

A flamingo is a tall, pink bird. It lives in shallow, salty lakes. All flamingos live in warm countries.

Flamingo families

Flamingos live in a huge group called a flock. There can be thousands of flamingos in the flock. Each pair of male and female flamingos builds a mud nest in shallow water. The female lays one egg. A baby flamingo, called a chick, hatches from the egg. Both parent birds take care of the chick until it is big enough to care for itself.

PLANT, INSECT, AND MEAT EATER

Flamingos eat insect larvae, small crabs, and shrimps. The pink shrimps give flamingos their pink color.

FLAMINGO FACTS

NUMBER OF KINDS	5
COLOR	pink or pinkish-gray
HEIGHT	up to 5 feet
LENGTH	up to 65 inches
WEIGHT	4–9 lbs.
STATUS	common
LIFE SPAN	about 10 years
ENEMIES	eagles, people

beak strains food from water

long neck to reach down into the water for food

long wings to help bird fly

long legs to wade through water and mud

a lesser flamingo

A female lesser flamingo cares for her chick.

Flea

see also: Insect

A flea is an insect. It lives on warm bodies of birds and mammals. It lives everywhere in the world. Fleas are pests. They suck blood from people and animals. They carry diseases.

Flea families

Adult fleas lay eggs in clothing. They lay eggs in animal nests and bedding. A young flea hatches into a larva. Then three weeks to eight months later the larva spins a cocoon. It is an adult when it comes out of the cocoon. The new adult flea quickly finds a mammal or bird on which to live.

MEAT EATER

An adult flea sucks the blood of the animal on which it lives. Flea larvae feed on fallen hair, food scraps and dirt.

FLEA FACTS

NUMBER OF KINDS	1,800
COLOR	black or brown
LENGTH	much less than one inch
STATUS	common
LIFE SPAN	nearly 2 years
ENEMIES	special chemicals called insecticides

hard body shell to protect the flea from the scratching animal

a cat flea

hard beak to pierce an animal's skin to suck its blood

spikes on legs to move quickly through fur and feathers

long, strong back legs to jump more than twelve inches from one animal to another

This cat flea larva is feeding on blood.

Flood

see also: Delta, River, Weather

A flood is when water flows over the land. Floods can ruin crops. Floods can damage buildings. Floods can wash away people and animals.

Types of flood

Sometimes extra water from melting snow or rain runs into rivers and streams. Then the rivers and streams overflow. Some of the flood water sinks into the soil. The rest of the flood water flows back into the river or dries up in the sun.

Seawater can also flood the land. Strong winds can cause big waves to come ashore and flood the land.

The Thames Barrier in London, England, protects the city from flood water.

Many rivers overflowed their banks during the 1993 floods in the Midwest United States.

People and floods

People have always lived near rivers. They use the rivers for transportation, fishing, and washing. The land along a river is good for farming, but rivers can flood the land. There are different ways to protect people from floods. Dams across rivers can hold back extra water. River banks and sea walls can be made higher and stronger. Special diggers called dredgers can make rivers deeper so that they hold more water.

Flower

see also: Leaf, Plants, Root, Seed, Stem

A flower is the part of a plant that produces seeds. Many flowers have brightly colored petals. Flowering plants grow almost everywhere on land. They do not grow in very cold places.

Life of a flower

The job of a flower is to make new plants. A flower can have male pollen, or it can have female ovules. One flower might have both. A grain of pollen from one flower joins with an ovule in another flower. This makes a seed. The seed might grow into a new plant.

Many people grow flowers. Some flowers are grown as a crop. Some flowers are grown to make perfume.

Sunflowers are grown as a crop. Sunflower seeds are used in animal feeds. The seeds are also crushed for their oil.

FLOWER FACTS

NUMBER OF KINDS OF FLOWERING PLANTS...............	more than 250 thousand
SIZE	up to 35 inches across
LIFESPAN	flowering plants can live more than 100 years
ENEMIES	fungi, bacteria, some insects

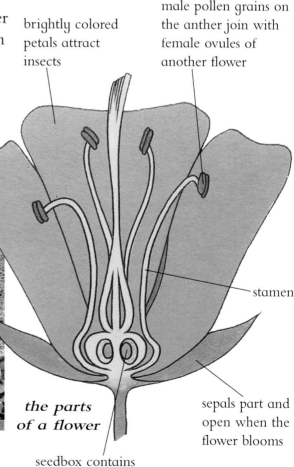

brightly colored petals attract insects

male pollen grains on the anther join with female ovules of another flower

stamen

the parts of a flower

seedbox contains ovules which become seeds

sepals part and open when the flower blooms

Fly

see also: Insect, Mosquito

A fly is an insect. Flies live all over the world. Many flies carry germs. The germs can cause food poisoning and diseases, such as malaria and sleeping sickness.

Fly families

A large group of flies is called a swarm. A fly begins life as an egg. The egg hatches into a maggot. It looks like a small worm. The full-grown maggot changes into a pupa. Then it changes into an adult fly.

FLY FACTS

NUMBER OF	
KINDS	about 100 thousand
COLOR	usually black, gray, brown, or yellowish
LENGTH	less than an inch to 3 inches
STATUS	common
LIFE SPAN	up to 2 years
ENEMIES	spiders, birds, people, chemicals called insecticides

a housefly

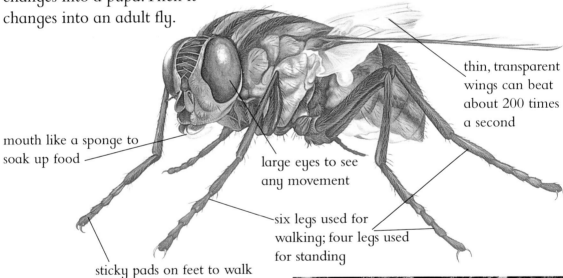

mouth like a sponge to soak up food

large eyes to see any movement

thin, transparent wings can beat about 200 times a second

six legs used for walking; four legs used for standing

sticky pads on feet to walk upside down on ceilings

MEAT EATER

Some flies, such as mosquitoes, bite their prey. Then they suck up a drop of the prey's blood. Other flies, such as houseflies, spit on their food. Then they suck up the spit mixed with the food.

These blowfly maggots are feeding.

Folk Music

see also: Music, Musical Instruments

The first folk music was the music played or sung by people every day. People have always liked to sing together as they worked. They like to listen to other people sing. Folk musicians usually play guitars, fiddles, flutes, and harps.

Folk music today

Today there are professional folk musicians. Their job is to play instruments and sing. Many folk musicians give concerts. Other people play just for fun.

New folk music

Many old folk songs are still popular. Songs and tunes are handed down year after year from one musician to another. Folk music has also changed over the years. People play old songs on new instruments. People find new ways of playing old tunes. People are always writing new folk music, too.

These musicians are playing at an outdoor folk music concert.

Every country in the world has its own folk music. These musicians are from the Andes Mountains in South America.

Cecil Sharp (1859–1924)

Cecil Sharp, an Englishman, came to the United States in 1916. He was very interested in old folk songs and dances. He collected songs from the people living in the Appalachian Mountains. The people were singing songs that immigrants had brought with them from England 300 years before. People in England no longer knew the tunes to some of these songs. Now the songs are in Sharp's books and everyone can sing and play them.

Food Chain

see also: Animals, Plants

Animals eat to get energy. Some animals eat plants. Some animals eat other animals. A food chain shows how the energy passes from one creature to another.

From plants to animals
The first link in all food chains starts with plants. Animals that eat plants are called herbivores. That is the next link. Animals called carnivores eat other animals. They are the next link.

People and the food chain
Humans are in food chains, too. Most humans are omnivores. They eat both plants and animals.

Lions are carnivores. They are trying to catch and eat the plant-eating wildebeests.

This shows a food chain. The sun helps the rosebush to grow. The aphids eat the bush. The ladybug eats the aphids. The bird eats the ladybug. The cat eats the bird.

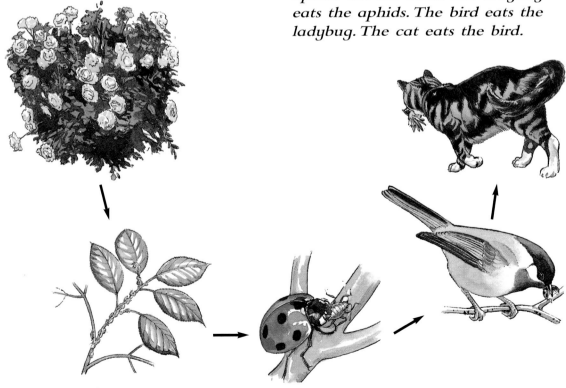

Forest

see also: Rainforest, Tree, Wood

A forest is where many trees grow close together. Forests cover more than one third of all the land on Earth. Forests are homes for many kinds of birds, animals, and insects.

Trees have been cut down in large parts of the Amazon rainforest. The treeless land is not always good for growing crops.

Types of forests

Forests in cold places mostly have coniferous trees. These are trees with needle leaves and cones. Fir and pine trees are coniferous. Forests in warm places mostly have deciduous trees. These are trees that have broad leaves that fall off once a year. Oak, elm, maple, and beech trees are deciduous trees. Tropical rainforests grow in places that are very hot and wet.

People and forests

Forests are important to people. Trees make oxygen that people, animals, and plants need to breathe.

People are cutting down forests to open up land for farming. They are cutting down trees to sell the wood. They are doing this without planting new trees. In many countries, the forests are nearly gone.

Forests can create an environment where other plants can live. This Eucalyptus forest in Australia is a good place for ferns to grow.

Fossil

see also: Dinosaur, Fuel

Fossils are formed from dead animals or plants. Looking at fossils tells us about animals and plants that lived a long time ago.

How fossils form

Plants leave behind leaves and stems. Animals leave behind bones or shells. What is left behind is covered with mud. When the mud turns to rock, the shape of the leaf, stem, bone, or shell stays in the rock. The shape in the rock is the fossil.

What fossils are found?

Some fossils are from creatures that are like animals that are still living today. Many fossils are from animals like dinosaurs that died out millions of years ago. Fossil bones tell us a lot about the size and shape of dinosaurs.

Coal is a fossil that people use as fuel. Coal is made from dead plants that have been squeezed hard and heated underground. Coal is called a fossil fuel.

DID YOU KNOW?

Chalk is a kind of fossil. It is made of the shells of tiny sea creatures that died millions of years ago.

This is a fossil of a fish. The fish lived 200 million years ago.

This scientist is working carefully on a rock with fossil remains. He can tell when the animals that made the fossils were alive.

Fox

see also: Coyote, Dog, Wolf

A fox is a mammal. It is a member of the dog family. Foxes are found almost everywhere north of the equator. The most common foxes are the red fox and the Arctic fox.

Fox families

A male is called a dog. A female is called a vixen. The babies are called cubs. A fox stays with its mate for its whole life. The vixen usually has four to five cubs at a time. Foxes dig a home called a den or earth. The dog fox usually hunts for food at night. The vixen looks after the cubs. Female cubs may stay with their parents for a year. Young males leave the den when they are about six months old.

FOX FACTS

NUMBER OF KINDS	21
COLOR	red, gray, or white
LENGTH	up to 32 inches
WEIGHT	about 22 lbs.
STATUS	common
LIFE SPAN	about 10 years
ENEMIES	People hunt foxes for sport and to protect chickens.

long, full tail to keep warm while sleeping

sensitive nose to smell food and danger

strong legs for running

long muzzle for carrying food

sharp claws for digging

an American red fox

MEAT EATERS

A fox eats rabbits and small rodents. It also eats birds and eggs. Foxes will take chickens from farms. In autumn, foxes will eat soft fruit.

A female red fox looks after her two cubs in their den. These foxes live in the mountains of Montana.

France

see also: Europe

France is a country in western Europe. France has high mountains in the east and southwest. There are also big areas of lowland. The lowland has wide, winding rivers.

Living in France

Most people live in towns and cities. Most of the land is farmland. Farmers grow grain and grapes. Cheese is made from cows' and goats' milk. France is well-known for its food and its cooking. French cheeses, wine, bread, and mineral water are sold all over the world.

Cars, aircraft, clothes, and other goods are made in factories.

The main French festival is Bastille Day on July 14. This festival celebrates the French Revolution in 1789.

DID YOU KNOW?

The Eiffel Tower was built in 1889. It is named after its designer, Gustave Eiffel.

The Eiffel Tower is a famous landmark in Paris.

EUROPE

FACT FILE

PEOPLE	French
POPULATION	58 million
MAIN LANGUAGE	French
CAPITAL CITY	Paris
MONEY	Euro
HIGHEST MOUNTAIN	Mont Blanc—15,777 feet
LONGEST RIVER	Loire River—633 miles

Frog

see also: Amphibian,
Metamorphosis, Toad

A frog is an amphibian. It is born
in the water but spends most of
its life on land. Different kinds of
frogs live all over the world. A
few frogs can climb trees. Most
frogs hide during the day. They
come out at night.

Frog families

A frog lays about 2,000–4,000 eggs in
spring. The eggs are laid in a pond. The
eggs are called frogspawn. These eggs
hatch as tadpoles. Most frogs do not take
care of their tadpoles. Over a few weeks
or months the tadpoles change into
frogs. Frogs in cold
countries hibernate
in mud or in leaves
during the
winter.

springy back legs
to jump

The dark spot in each egg can
turn into a tadpole.

FROG FACTS

NUMBER OF KINDS	about 2,600
COLOR	Poisonous frogs are brightly colored. Most other frogs are brown or green.
LENGTH	up to 12 inches
STATUS	common
LIFE SPAN	5 to 12 years
ENEMIES	Foxes, herons, fish, and ducks eat frogs. Ducks, newts, and dragonfly larvae eat tadpoles.

eyes that look two ways
for danger

long, sticky
tongue to
catch insects

webbed feet for
swimming

an American
river frog

PLANT, INSECT, AND MEAT EATER

Tadpoles eat water weeds. Bigger
tadpoles eat insects. Adult frogs eat
flies and slugs.

Fuel

see also: Electricity, Energy, Fossil

A fuel is anything that gives off heat or other energy. Natural gas, oil, and coal are all fuels.

Types of fuel

Natural gas is underground. A deep hole, called a well, is drilled into the ground. The gas rushes up out of the hole. Gas is used for cooking and heating. It is also used for making electricity in a power plant.

Oil is often found in the same places as gas. Crude oil is pumped from underground. Gasoline, diesel fuel, and heating oil all come from crude oil.

Coal comes from the ground. Most of it is burned in power plants to make electricity.

DID YOU KNOW?

In some places people use a machine that makes fuel out of cow manure.

Peat is partly decayed plant matter. It is dug from the ground and dried. Peat can be burned as fuel.

People and fuels

One day all the fuels in the ground will be used up. Scientists are trying to find ways to use fuels that will not run out. These are renewable fuels. Two sources of renewable energy are the sun and the wind. They will not run out like fossil fuels from the ground.

This is an oil refinery in Kuwait. An oil refinery turns black, sticky crude oil into useful fuel.

Fungus

see also: Plants

A fungus is a living thing. It is like a plant, but it does not have leaves, stems, or real roots. Fungi include mushrooms, toadstools, yeasts, and molds. Fungi grow almost everywhere. They grow on land and in water.

FUNGI FACTS

NUMBER OF	
KINDS	about 100 thousand
LARGEST FUNGI	up to 12 inches across
LIFE SPAN	up to many years
ENEMIES	bacteria, special chemicals called fungicides

a rainforest fungus

Life of a fungus

The main part of the fungus is under the ground. Tiny threads take in food from the soil. A mushroom is the fruit of a fungus. A fungus produces spores instead of seeds. The spores are scattered by the wind or by animals. Some fungi grow on living plants and animals.

gills underneath the mushroom contain spores

Some fungi cause diseases in people, animals, and plants. Other fungi are useful. Fungi make bread rise. They make yogurt and some cheeses. Fungi also make the medicine called penicillin. Some mushrooms can be eaten. Other mushrooms and toadstools are poisonous.

Tiny fungi grow in forest leaf litter. Scientists who study fungi are called mycologists.

Germany

see also: Europe

Germany is a country in the middle of Europe. The north of Germany is lowland. The center and south have hills and mountains. Big rivers flow through Germany from south to north. The weather is mostly warm in summer. It can be very cold with snow in winter.

Living in Germany

Most Germans live and work in its big cities.

There are special traditions and festivals in most towns and villages. Some festivals are 600 years old. One of the most famous festivals reminds people of the "Pied Piper of Hamelin." The pied piper is believed to have led the rats out of the town of Hamelin.

DID YOU KNOW?

From 1949 to 1990 Germany was divided into two countries. The western half was called the German Federal Republic and the eastern half was the German Democratic Republic.

Many towns and cities in Germany have open squares. This open square is in the Romer area of Frankfurt.

EUROPE

FACT FILE

PEOPLE	Germans
POPULATION	about 80 million
MAIN LANGUAGE	German
CAPITAL CITY	Berlin
MONEY	Euro
HIGHEST MOUNTAIN	Zugspitze–9,725 feet
LONGEST RIVER	Rhine River–820 miles

Ghana

see also: Africa

Ghana is a country in west Africa. It is mostly hot lowland. It is cooler in the hills in the east and west. The world's largest man-made lake is in Ghana. It is called Lake Volta.

Living in Ghana

Most people in Ghana live near the coast. More than half of the people work on farms.

Rice, yams, and cassava are grown. They are eaten with meat, fish, and peanut stews. Many Ghanaians wear clothes made of *kente*. This is a special, many-colored cloth. The cloth is sold in the markets. It is also sold to other countries.

Ghana also has small factories and mines. The cocoa beans they grow are sent all over the world to be made into chocolate.

Traders sell their produce in local markets. This market is in Kasoa, in the center of Ghana.

DID YOU KNOW?

Ghana was once part of an area called the Gold Coast. It took the name *Ghana* when it became an independent country in 1957.

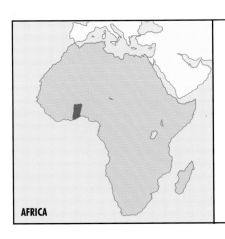

AFRICA

FACT FILE

PEOPLE	Ghanaians
POPULATION	about 17 million
MAIN LANGUAGES	English, African languages
CAPITAL CITY	Accra
MONEY	Cedi
HIGHEST MOUNTAIN	Mt. Afadjado—2,905 feet
LONGEST RIVER	Volta River—950 miles

Giraffe

see also: Mammal

A giraffe is the tallest land mammal in the world. It lives on the grassy plains of Africa. Every giraffe has a different color pattern.

male giraffe's horns used for fighting

A giraffe spreads its legs and bends low to get a drink.

long tongue to pull leaves from trees

Giraffe families

A male giraffe is called a bull. A female giraffe is called a cow. A cow has one baby at a time. The baby is called a calf. The females look after each other's babies. Giraffes do not stay in one special group. They move from group to group. They do not build a home. Bull giraffes fight. The winner of the fight becomes the head bull.

GIRAFFE FACTS

NUMBER OF KINDS	1
COLOR	brown, yellow, and white
LENGTH	about 6 feet
HEIGHT	up to 17 feet
WEIGHT	up to 4,200 lbs.
STATUS	endangered
LIFE SPAN	about 25 years
ENEMIES	Hyenas, leopards, and wild dogs

long neck to reach high into trees

patterned coat for hiding

tail to swish away insects

a giraffe

PLANT EATER

A giraffe eats leaves and shoots from tall trees. It also eats grass.

Goat

see also: Mammal

A goat is a medium-sized mammal. People keep goats for their milk, meat, and wool. Wild goats live in some mountain areas.

Goat families

A male goat is called a billy goat or a buck. A female goat is called a nanny goat or a doe. A nanny goat usually has two babies at a time. A young goat is called a kid. Farm goats are kept together in groups called herds.

GOAT FACTS

NUMBER OF KINDS	600 (mainly farm goats)
COLOR	brown, black, white
HEIGHT	18 inches to 4 feet
WEIGHT	20 to 300 lbs.
STATUS	common
LIFE SPAN	8 to 10 years
ENEMIES	wolves, bears, lions, leopards

horns for fighting

billy and nanny goats may have beards

shaggy hair that can be woven into wool

an American mountain goat

strong legs to climb steep cliffs

Mountain goats are very sure-footed. Even the very young goats can safely trot along narrow ledges.

PLANT EATER

A goat eats all kinds of plants and fruit. It even eats spiky thorn bushes. Farm goats will eat almost anything. They will even eat the labels off tin cans.

Goose

see also: Bird

A goose is a large bird. It lives near water in all but the coldest parts of the world. Some geese are raised by farmers. Geese are raised for their meat, eggs, and feathers.

Goose families

A male is called a gander. A female is called a goose. A baby is called a gosling. The gander and goose build a nest on the ground. They fill the nest with grass. The goose lays from three to eleven eggs. After the eggs hatch, both parents feed the goslings.

Many kinds of geese migrate long distances. They travel each fall to spend the winter in warmer places. They travel in groups called flocks. The flock flies in a big V-shape. The geese take turns being the leader of the flock.

GOOSE FACTS

NUMBER OF KINDS	more than 30
COLOR	usually gray, white, or black
LENGTH	up to 4 feet
WEIGHT	up to 11 lbs.
STATUS	common
LIFE SPAN	up to 20 years
ENEMIES	foxes, people

sharp-edged beak for cutting grass

waterproof feathers for swimming

strong wings for flying and fighting

webbed feet for swimming

a Canada goose

PLANT EATER

A goose eats plants found in the water and on land.

Snow goose goslings keep warm in a nest lined with their mother's down feathers.

Grasshopper

see also: Insect

A grasshopper is an insect. It uses its long back legs to jump. It rubs its legs or wings to make a clicking or whirring noise. Grasshoppers live in most parts of the world. They do not live in the Arctic or Antarctica.

Grasshopper families

A grasshopper lays its eggs in the soil. A young grasshopper hatches from the egg. The young grasshopper is called a larva. The larva grows and sheds its skin many times. It slowly changes into an adult with wings. Big groups of grasshoppers are called swarms.

GRASSHOPPER FACTS

NUMBER OF KINDS	about 10 thousand
COLOR	usually green
LENGTH	up to 4 inches
STATUS	common
LIFE SPAN	up to about 9 months
ENEMIES	birds, snakes, frogs, spiders, beetles, people

PLANT EATER

Some grasshoppers eat only one kind of plant. Others eat any plant they find.

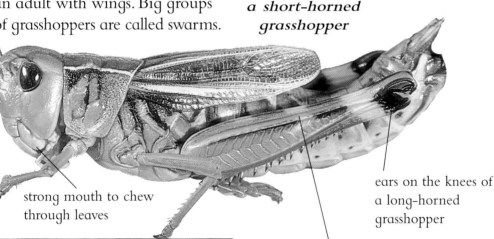

a short–horned grasshopper

long antennae to smell and feel

strong mouth to chew through leaves

ears on the knees of a long-horned grasshopper

long back legs to jump almost 40 times its own length

These young grasshoppers have a bright warning color. The color may keep away predators.

Greece

see also: Europe; Greece, Ancient

Greece is a country in southeast Europe. Greece has many islands in the Mediterranean Sea.

Living in Greece

Half of the people of Greece live in small towns and villages. Many houses are painted white. The white color reflects the hot sun. This helps keep the inside cool. Olives, grapes, potatoes, and sugar beets are grown on small farms.

People from all over the world visit Greece. They enjoy the hot, sunny summers. They visit the ruins of Ancient Greece. Many Greeks work in hotels and museums. Some Greeks have boats to carry people and goods between the many islands.

Many small fishing boats work around the Greek coast and islands.

DID YOU KNOW?

Greece has a big shipping fleet. Ships from Greece sail all over the world. They carry goods such as grain and oil.

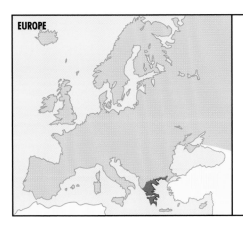

FACT FILE

PEOPLE . . . . Greeks

POPULATION . . . . about 10 million

MAIN LANGUAGE . . . . Greek

CAPITAL CITY . . . . Athens

MONEY . . . . Euro

HIGHEST MOUNTAIN . . . . Mount Olympus–9,574 feet

LONGEST RIVER . . . . Aliakmon River–180 miles

Greece, Ancient

see also: Greece, Olympic Games

The civilization of Ancient Greece began about 800 B.C. It lasted until about 146 B.C. when the Romans began to take over.

What were the Ancient Greeks like?

The Ancient Greeks lived in city-states. A city-state was a city and the land around the city. Each city-state had its own government. Some city-states had one leader. In other city-states the men voted. They decided how to run the government. All men had to fight when a city-state went to war. Women stayed home with the children.

The Ancient Greeks believed in and prayed to many gods and goddesses. The people gave the gods and goddesses presents to keep them happy.

For what are the Ancient Greeks known?

The Ancient Greeks are well-known for their buildings, statues, and painted vases. Ancient Greek thinkers, writers, and inventors are still studied and remembered.

KEY DATES

800 B.C.	states begin
776 B.C.	first Olympic Games held
700 B.C.	Greek alphabet invented
400 B.C	Greeks begin to use mathematics
336–323 B.C.	Alexander the Great rules all of Greece
146 B.C.	Greece becomes part of the Roman Empire

The ancient ruins of the Acropolis are in the city of Athens. The Acropolis was a group of buildings on a hill. The largest building was the temple called the Parthenon.

Guatemala

see also: North America

Guatemala is a country in central America. There are lowlands near the coast and in the north. Mountains cross the middle of Guatemala. The mountains have very rich soil. There are also active volcanoes in the mountains. Rainforest covers the northern part of the country.

Living in Guatemala

Most people in Guatemala live in small towns and villages. They live where the soil is good for farming. The farmers grow coffee, sugar, bananas, corn, and beans. The chicozapunte tree grows in the northern rainforest. The sap of this tree is used to make chewing gum.

The people in Guatemala eat mixed beans and rice. They eat salads made of avocados, tomatoes, and onions. The bread they eat is made from corn.

Mayan people weave brightly colored cloth and rugs.

DID YOU KNOW?

More than 1,000 years ago, northern Guatemala was part of the ancient Mayan civilization. Even today most of the people are Mayan Indians.

NORTH AMERICA

FACT FILE

PEOPLE................... Guatemalans
POPULATION .... about 10 million
MAIN LANGUAGE .... Spanish
CAPITAL CITY .... Guatemala City
MONEY .... Quetzal
HIGHEST MOUNTAIN ... Volcán Tajumulco–13,840 feet
LONGEST RIVER........ Rio Salinas–298 miles

Gull

see also: Bird, Seabird

A gull is a sea bird. A gull can fly. It can float on water. A gull cannot dive underwater. Many gulls move away from the sea. They live on lakes or rivers. Gulls are found all over the world.

Gull families

Gulls choose a partner. The partners usually stay together for life. Some gulls build round nests on the beach. Other gulls lay eggs on cliff ledges. A female gull lays two or three eggs once a year. A baby gull is called a chick. Both parents feed the chick. A chick pecks at the adults' beaks to let them know it needs food.

GULL FACTS

NUMBER OF KINDS	43
COLOUR	white, gray, and black
LENGTH	up to 26 inches
STATUS	common
LIFE SPAN	about 30 years
ENEMIES	rats, people

curved beak to pull off bits of food

a herring gull

waterproof feathers to keep dry

webbed feet for walking on sand and paddling through water

Herring gull chicks have splotchy markings. The markings help it hide from enemies.

PLANT, INSECT, AND MEAT EATER

A gull eats almost anything it finds. It even eats the meat of dead seals and whales. A gull breaks open the hard shells of mussels and crabs by dropping the shells to the ground from the sky.

Haiti

see also: North America

Haiti is a country. It is on part of the island of Hispaniola. It is in the Caribbean Sea. Haiti has mountains with small valleys. It has hot coastal plains. The climate is hot and wet all year round.

Living in Haiti

Most people in Haiti live in the country. They live on very small farms. They grow coffee, sisal, sugar cane, and cocoa. These crops are sold to other countries. Farmers also grow corn, cassava, sweet potatoes, and beans. Cloth is made in factories.

The life style of the people is called Creole. Creole is a mix of African and French life styles. The food, houses, and music are Creole. The people follow both old African religions and Christianity.

Haiti has a carnival time. The people dress in costumes. They dance through the streets in big parades.

DID YOU KNOW?

King Christophe of Haiti began using gourds as money about 200 years ago. A gourd is a hard-skinned fruit. It is like a pumpkin. Haiti uses coins now, but they still call the money *gourde*.

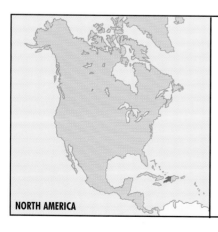

NORTH AMERICA

FACT FILE

PEOPLE	Haitians
POPULATION	7 million
MAIN LANGUAGES	French, Haitian Creole
CAPITAL CITY	Port-au-Prince
MONEY	Gourde
HIGHEST MOUNTAIN	Chaîne de la Selle—8,796 feet
LONGEST RIVER	Artibonite River—100 miles

Hare

see also: Mammal, Rabbits

A hare is a mammal. It looks like a rabbit. It has long ears and long legs. Hares are also called jackrabbits. Hares live on grassland. Hares that live in snowy places have white fur in the winter.

Hare families

A male hare is called a jack. A female hare is called a doe. The doe has from two to four babies at a time. The babies are called leverets. The doe scrapes a small hollow in the grass. The nest is called a form. The doe puts grass in the form to make it soft. She makes a form for each leveret after they are born. The leverets leave their mother when they are three weeks old. Then they live on their own.

These European hare leverets are warming themselves in the sun.

HARE FACTS

NUMBER OF KINDS	44 hares and rabbits
COLOR	brown, gray, or white
LENGTH	about 24 inches
WEIGHT	about 11 lbs.
STATUS	common
LIFE SPAN	about 5 years
ENEMIES	foxes, eagles

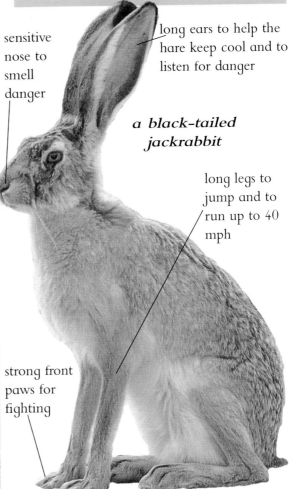

sensitive nose to smell danger

long ears to help the hare keep cool and to listen for danger

a black-tailed jackrabbit

long legs to jump and to run up to 40 mph

strong front paws for fighting

PLANT EATER

A hare feeds at night on grass, roots, bark, and grain.

Hawk

see also: Bird

A hawk is a bird of prey. It catches and kills animals to eat. There are many kinds of hawks. They live all over the world except in Antarctica.

Hawk families

A female hawk lays eggs in a nest. The chicks hatch and stay in the nest. They are fed by the parent birds until they can fly. Hawk nests can be on a cliff, in a tree, or on the ground.

HAWK FACTS

NUMBER OF KINDS	about 200
COLOR	usually brown or gray
LENGTH	10 to 28 inches
WEIGHT	3 oz. to 4 lbs.
STATUS	common
LIFE SPAN	up to 25 years
ENEMIES	larger birds, people

broad wings to soar through the air

good eyesight to spot small animals from high in the air

sharp, hooked beak to tear up food

curved talons to grasp and carry prey

tail to steer while soaring

a buzzard

The crested hawk feeds her chicks insects and frogs.

INSECT AND MEAT EATER

Hawks eat mice, frogs, insects, and other small animals. Some hawks swallow the whole animal. Then they bring it up and spit out the fur, feathers, and bones.

Heart

see also: Blood, Human Body

The heart is a special, strong muscle. It is a pump. It pumps blood around the body. Every animal has a heart. It is in the chest of most animals.

How the heart works

The heart has four spaces. The top two spaces are called atria. They fill up with blood that has gone around the body through the veins. The atria squeeze the blood into the two spaces at the bottom of the heart. These spaces are called the ventricles. Valves in the heart let the blood go only in one direction. The valves are like doors that only open one way.

A human heart beats more than two billion times in a lifetime. The heart pumps slowly when a person is asleep. The heart pumps quickly when a person exercises.

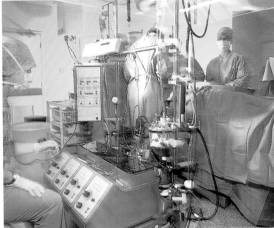

Doctors can perform operations on unhealthy hearts. Special machines do the work of the heart and lungs while the doctor operates.

STAY HEALTHY!

Eating the right food, not smoking, and getting plenty of exercise can keep the heart healthy.

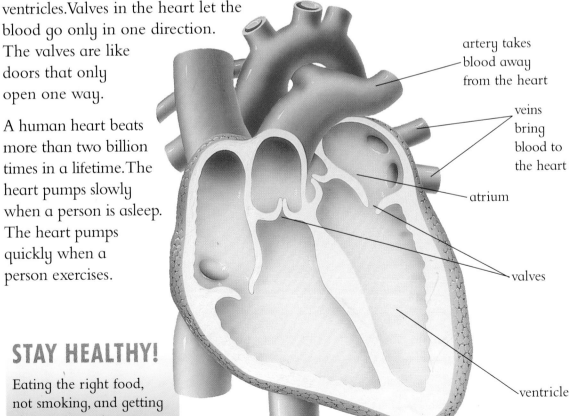

artery takes blood away from the heart

veins bring blood to the heart

atrium

valves

ventricle

the human heart

Heat

see also: Energy, Fuel

Heat is a kind of energy. Heat is usually released by burning fuel. There are many types of fuel. Firewood and the food we eat are fuels.

Types of heat

Heat is important to human beings. A person can die if the body is not warm enough.

Materials called insulators keep in heat. Curtains that cover windows help to keep heat inside a house. Warm clothing in winter helps to keep a person's body from losing heat. The fur on an animal is also a very good insulator.

A special camera shows heat escaping from a house. The yellow areas show where the most heat is escaping.

Materials called conductors allow heat to escape. Metals are good conductors.

People and heat

People have used heat to cook food and for warmth since humans first made fires a long time ago. Heat can also soften or melt things in order to change their shape. Metals and some plastics are shaped this way.

Pots and pans are made of a conductor such as metal. The heat passes from the burner to the food. The handle is made of an insulator. This protects a person's hand from the heat.

Hedgehog

see also: Hibernation, Mammal

A hedgehog is a mammal. A hedgehog's body is covered in spines. A hedgehog rolls into a ball to protect itself from danger. Hedgehogs are found in woods and fields. They are found in parts of Europe, Asia, Africa, and New Zealand.

Hedgehog families

The male lives on his own. The female builds a special nest in spring or summer. She has from four to six babies. The babies leave the nest after four weeks. Hedgehogs that live in cold places hibernate all winter.

HEDGEHOG FACTS

NUMBER OF KINDS	12
COLOR	brown
LENGTH	8 to 12 inches
WEIGHT	about 25 oz.
STATUS	common
LIFE SPAN	about 6 years
ENEMIES	foxes, people

good ears to hear worms and insects

special eyes to see at night

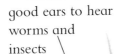

a European hedgehog

long nose to find food on the ground

sharp spines to protect from danger

little feet can be tucked inside to roll into a ball

Hedgehog babies are born with soft spines that quickly harden.

PLANT AND INSECT EATER

A hedgehog hunts for worms and insects at night. It also likes to eat soft fruit.

Helicopter

see also: Airplane, Transportation

A helicopter is an aircraft without fixed wings. A helicopter has spinning blades called rotors. The rotors are on top of the helicopter. The rotors push the helicopter up into the air.

The first helicopters

Helicopters were first thought of hundreds of years ago. The first helicopter was built in 1907. It easily went out of control. Helicopters improved and could fly by 1937. The United States Army was the first to use helicopters. Most helicopters are still used by the military.

How we use helicopters

Helicopters can land almost anywhere. They can take off straight up into the air. They can go forwards, backwards, and sideways. They can hover over the same spot. These movements make them very useful. They can land where there is no room for an airplane to land. Helicopters rescue people from sinking ships or mountain cliffs. Helicopters are used as ambulances. They are used by the police to chase criminals.

HELICOPTER FIRSTS

INVENTED	1907
FIRST MILITARY HELICOPTERS	1942
FIRST PASSENGER HELICOPTER	1945
FIRST TRANSATLANTIC HELICOPTER FLIGHT	1967

In 1907, Paul Cornu's double rotor machine crashed almost every time it tried to take off.

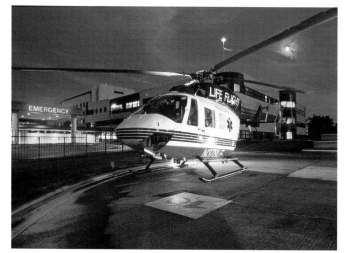

An ambulance helicopter can travel very quickly to places that other vehicles cannot reach.

Hibernation

see also: Animals, Seasons

Some animals have a type of winter sleep. It is called hibernation. Animals hibernate in the winter because there is not much food available when it is cold. The animal wakes up when the weather gets warmer.

What is hibernation?

Hibernation is more than just going to sleep. First, hibernating animals need to eat a lot before hibernating. The fat on their bodies will keep them alive while they sleep. They also need to hide in a safe place where enemies can't find them. While hibernating, the animal's heartbeat slows down. The animal's breathing is very shallow and slow. The animal almost looks dead. It can take days for the animal to become fully awake.

Black bears have a long winter sleep that looks like hibernation.

Who hibernates?

Many different kinds of animals hibernate. Butterflies and other insects will sometimes hibernate in sheds and garages. Bats hibernate in caves and roofs where they roost. Snakes and other reptiles also hibernate. Frogs and toads bury themselves in mud or piles of leaves.

Some animals are only hiding in the winter. They are not really hibernating. Squirrels stay in their nests. They rest for most of the winter. They come out on fine, warm days.

This hedgehog has been hibernating under a pile of leaves.

Hieroglyphics

see also: Alphabet, Aztecs, Egypt, Ancient; Maya

Hieroglyphics are a kind of writing. Hieroglyphics use pictures. All ancient styles of writing used hieroglyphics.

Who used hieroglyphics?

The Ancient Egyptians, the Mayas, and the Aztecs all used hieroglyphics. They carved them on stone. They painted them on stone or paper.

Hieroglyphics showed real things. It was hard to show ideas. Drawing or carving hieroglyphics took a long time. They were hard to learn. The pictures had to be drawn nearly the same way each time. Only a few people could read or write hieroglyphics.

What happened to hieroglyphics?

People who used hieroglyphics began to change the pictures. They made the pictures stand for sounds. The sound pictures were used to spell words. Later, alphabets replaced hieroglyphics. Alphabets could express words more clearly. Alphabets were quicker and easier to learn.

KEY DATES

4000 B.C.	first alphabet is used
3000 B.C.	Egyptians begin to use hieroglyphics
A.D. 500	Maya begin to use hieroglyphics
A.D. 1200	Aztecs begin to use hieroglyphics

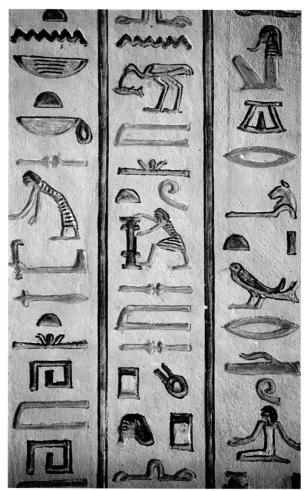

Hieroglyphics on a tomb told something about the person inside.

Hinduism

see also: India

Hinduism is the oldest world religion. It began in India about 4,000 years ago. Its followers are called Hindus.

Beliefs and teachings

Hindus believe that everyone has duties. The duties are called dharma. Dharma includes things like worshiping God and not hurting other people. Hindus believe it is important to lead a good life.

Hindus believe in a great power called Brahman. They worship Brahman through many gods. Two important gods are Shiva and Vishnu. Each Hindu god has special powers. They have powers over things like money or childbirth. The Hindu beliefs and teachings are written in holy books called the *Vedas*.

This statue of a Hindu god is decorated with flowers.

Hinduism today

There are over 700 million Hindus in the world. Nearly half of them live in India. Hindus worship and pray in their homes and at temples. There are many important Hindu festivals. One festival is Divali. It is the festival of lights. This is when Hindus celebrate stories of the gods overcoming evil.

Festivals are important in Hinduism. The one shown here is honoring the god Shiva.

Hippopotamus

see also: Mammal

A hippopotamus is a very heavy land mammal. Only the elephant is heavier. Hippopotamuses live in central Africa. Hippopotamuses stay in water during the day. They come out of the water to eat grass at night when it is cooler.

Hippopotamus families

A baby hippo can swim and walk as soon as it is born. A mother and her young may live together for several years. They live in a group of fifteen to twenty hippos. Each group has one adult male. Other adult males live together in their own groups.

HIPPOPOTAMUS FACTS

NUMBER OF KINDS	2
COLOR	brown
LENGTH	up to 11 feet
HEIGHT	5 feet
WEIGHT	up to 7,000 lbs.
STATUS	common
LIFE SPAN	up to 50 years
ENEMIES	Crocodiles sometimes kill baby hippos.

a hippopotamus

eyes, ears, and nose on top to see, hear, and breathe when in the water

short, wide legs hold up this heavy animal when it is on land

big teeth for fighting; little teeth for munching grass

PLANT EATER

A hippopotamus can walk as much as two miles every night to look for fresh grass.

Hippos wallow in water during the day. The baby hippos are kept safe on top of the adults.